HOW AVERAGE PEOPLE TOOK ON THE WALL STREET WITH GAMESTOP

TITUS SOFRON
AUTHOR

WALLSTREETBETS QUICK STORY

The story of how average Joe's squeezed GameStop and Wall Street into submission!

Titus Sofron

Key Solutions Management of Alaska, LLC

CONTENTS

CHAPTER I

Overview of the book

The New York Stock Exchange, or NYSE, is the world's largest stock market in terms of market capitalization – a whopping 30 trillion USD as of February 2018. The stock exchange sees the transaction of share volumes anywhere between 2 and 6 billion a day. Thus its "Big Board" nickname is an understatement.

It is noteworthy that the NYSE is the territory of an elite class of traders, brokers, and all sorts of financial institutions known to the world collectively as "Wall Street." The name comes from Wall Street situated less than a quarter of a mile away from the NYSE, which was once the front desk for almost all the major financial institutions and investors of the NYSE. However, the sad reality regarding this high-functioning system is that its transactions and derived profits are typically accumulated in the accounts and portfolios of Wall Street's big wheel players on almost all the Stock Exchanges around the world.

Whenever the market opens to a possible trend, these big players set out tapping all the prospective strategies for profit. Sometimes they even go out of their way by sending in all their wild cards in the form of money, news, influence, or even insider trading just to create such situations that are favorable to their schemes. Pump and Dump is one such practice employed by unethical tycoons and is a form of investment fraud. Other unscrupulous practices kept mushrooming up over time as the stock markets have grown. Such conspiracies and schemes may be as old as the concept of the stock market and investments themselves.

Each time a big game takes center stage, the common trader or retailers take's losses. The money these big players make through such plans come from the wallets of the average man on the street breaking a sweat to fetch their family something more than just bread and butter that evening. When retailer investors enter the big seas most of the time, they turn into adventurers that are sailing into choppy, rough waters with this glimmer of hope that something will come out of their hard-earned money. Unfortunately, a happy conclusion doesn't happen all the time.

Post-war times, inflations, epidemics, pandemics, and market crashes, in [3]particular, have all led to unemployment in the past. In such situations, the people who were laid off or fired from their jobs looked for alternate ways to make money – and some of them ended up in stock markets – and then became prey to such money-hunts.

The 2008 Great Recession was one such major event that rattled the world. This global financial crisis that happened between 2007 and 2009 had funneled many middle income families who were being crushed under debt into the crazy world of stock markets. Most of them were crushed further when clever elites outwitted them on several occasions, but the elites were bailed out by the federal government because they were too big to fail. Many families even risked bankruptcy which resulted in their dependency to get different loans.

Pushing aside the adverse effects of the crisis, the last thirteen years taught them many lessons – including the fact that some losses will pay off. In this regard, the youngest (and once the least fortunate) of this generation were forged in too many hardships to be pinned down by losses or to be held back from a grueling challenge.

For many reasons, we could say that these hard-learned philosophies paid off now in January 2021, when the smaller fish, who were otherwise destined to be baited, gathered to temporarily gulp in the whales or the big players.

And in many ways, this was a sort of laidback throwback-payback too. The New York Stock Market became the center stage for marginalized retailers to steal the spotlight and prove their tenacity.

This book is a most humble attempt to look at the events under a different light, from a different perspective, and comprehend this anomaly, that could never have been foreseen or expected to happen. We will begin by looking at the fundamentals needed to break down this event. Next, we will delve deeper into the "whats", "whos", "whens", and "whys" of the event. Then we will proceed into the event itself – the big "HOW?" After that, we will hit the deeper waters to fathom how these little fish managed to take down these whales with all the gadgets and cameras.

Let's soak in the basics now, because you will be sitting on the edge of your seat.

CHAPTER II

*Stock Market 101 for anyone who
wants to study the GameStop
Short Squeeze 2020*

The terms Stock Market, Stock Exchange, and Equity Market all refer to the system of people and business firms trading the financial shares of companies that are listed under the so-called "market." By "listing" or the process known as Initial Public Offering or IPO, the companies offer a portion of their money for the general public to trade in relatively small quantities known as shares, stocks, or equity.

In the centuries of this process, the different transactions, advanced financial research, economic growth (and occasional declines), the prospects for development in the fields, governmental involvement, and the enlightenment of the masses regarding these topics, along with several incomprehensible factors had led to the development of something known today as Market Derivatives. These derivatives are also tradable under their specified rules.

In Simpler Terms...

To understand this concept, let us hypothetically equate an

entrepreneur to a dairy farmer who has successfully raised his farm (the listed company). Say he has a decent number of cows, which is equivalent to the market cap with each cow being a share. By this analogy, let the milk be the value or the price of the stock and other products to be the derivatives.

The farm is growing by the day in terms of the number of cows and products. Now the farmer thinks, "Hey! Maybe this many cows is too much for me to manage. If I had more time and money, I could have facilitated better care for more cows."

So, he puts up a board outside his farm saying he has decided to lend people half of his cows to raise. If they take care of them, they can have the products and whatever income they can make out of them; but the cow is never theirs.

Now, this plan is not just the farmer's way of ensuring his assets are taken care of - the farmer can now make more money from the people leasing out and use the money to make his business flourish even more in terms of infrastructure – just like the company raises funds through an IPO. Hypothetically speaking, now all the people who come and take up the cows are going to try and increase the value of their stock price. They are the institutional and retail buyers in this context. This is the just the beginning of the story, let's dive deeper.

How Does The Stock Market Function?

The Stock Market, as we discussed, is not a definable entity; but an inexplicable one. The boundaries of it cannot be drawn because each stock market practically involves hundreds of companies, millions of traders, billions of consumers of the companies, the government and its financial agencies, currencies, and influences from outside of a nation or market. The processes that are engaged day and night in accordance with the market and its growth may be daunting, but scalable.

The event that shook Wall Street occurred from something similarly trivial. To understand the highly debatable Reddit initiative from the group of users from the WallStreetBets community, we will be looking at a few expressions and other important information. Note that this is not the complete guide, but only the very important terms you need to know in order to comprehend this event.

The "Very Basics Of Stock Market Basics" To Shed Light On The Wallstreetbets Reddit Revolution.

Buying and selling of stocks and their derivatives are the elementary transactions that have sustained the markets over these centuries.

What Is A "Buy"?

It is the act of giving the price (at the moment) of a stock to acquire it. This is also referred to as taking a "position" because you are effectively becoming a partner of the company by buying a share of their finances. Now, if the company does well in either their business or in the equity market, or both, then you too get a profit known as "dividend." But if the company performs poorly, the price of the stock drops from the price you bought it for, and thus you share the losses.

What Is A "Sell"?

By selling a stock, you hand over the stock to another trader, but not back to the company. We will learn why when we discuss "Public Float." The price of the stock when you sell it is yours.

What Is A Candlestick Chart?

Candlestick charts originated in Japan over 100 years before the West developed the bar and point-and-figure charts. In the 1700s, a Japanese man named Homma discovered that, while there was a link between price and the supply and demand of rice, the markets were strongly influenced by the emotions of traders.[1]

Candlesticks show that emotion by visually representing the size of price moves with different colors. Traders use the candlesticks to make trading decisions based on regularly occurring patterns that help forecast the short-term direction of the price.

What Is Meant By "Holding A Position"?

Holding a position or stock refers to buying a share at a price with the anticipation that its price would go up and waiting without selling it.

Who Is A "Stockbroker"?

A stockbroker used to be a person who goes to the stock exchange for you and sorts out the paperwork and transactions of money and stocks for you. Today, a stockbroker could be a person, a financial service firm, or a digital financial platform that facilitates all sorts of stock market transactions. The services may or may not include bits of advice.

The Bulls, The Bearish, And The Market

When the price of a stock goes up, the particular stock is said to be "bullish" because the price is then controlled by the stock market participants who are buying the shares for higher and higher prices. Such strong buyers are called "Bulls" based on the way they affect, or attack, the market like a bull that strikes upward starting from the ground.

A "bullish market" is a market or the weighted value of a collection of stocks that goes up. It also is an indication that the market economy is growing.

By the same token, a bear attacks with downward strikes, pinning the foe down. So, when the price of a stock goes down, it is said to be "bearish." The traders selling are now leaving their mark on the market in red and this means the "bearish market" is going down.

What Is The "Public Float" Of A Stock?

When a company decides to enlist themselves for an IPO, a portion of their shares are made available to the public to trade at their liberty.

Remember the farmer we were talking about before? Public market float is the number of cows he decided to lease out.

The floating stock quantities are balanced out because when a buyer buys, a seller somewhere else sells. This term will come in handy as soon as we begin discussing the reason why as well as how a group of Redditors was able to make the moguls of Wall Street have a taste of their own medicine.

Trading Volume

Trading volume for a specific time period is the total number of shares that are being transacted (bought or sold). The trading volume tends to be higher when there is a significant change in the price of a stock.

"Liquidity" And "Volatility" Of Stocks

Just as the term suggests, the liquidity of a stock tells you how freely it can flow in or out of your portfolio. A liquid stock is one that has enough buyers and sellers, which enables us to buy or sell stocks at our own will. It also indicates the number of outstanding shares available. If a stock is liquid, it means that there are enough stocks to supply as per concurrent demand.

"Volatility" is a term that suggests something like its common meaning, just not in the same sense. A volatile stock is a stock that shows significant and unforeseeable changes in the stock price in either direction.

Volatility represents the extent of price change; whereas, liquidity is the ease of buying or selling a stock. While a liquid stock poses not many grave risks, trading in a volatile market falls along the lines of gambling. Liquid stocks are also the stocks of which buying demand and selling supply balance each other.

When this equilibrium is not more or less maintained, people or institutional investors may find loopholes in the system, sometimes for the worse and sometimes for the better.

What Are "Long Trades," "Short Trades," And "Stock Borrowing?" Why Is Every Beginner Trying To Learn These Terms?

Ever since you start looking at a candlestick charts, you will try and guess where the pattern is going – it may go up or it may go down (it can also go sideways, as you would know, but let's do up and down for now).

When a trader anticipates, for a variety of reasons, that the price of the stock may significantly go up (they expect a bullish market), they may buy a stock for the smallest price possible and wait until the price goes up. This is known as a Long Trade, and this is straightforward.

However, when the trader expects a drop in the price of a stock, what would they do? The stock markets had sorted this out over the years and developed a technique exclusive to the market.

This process involves a trader borrowing the required shares from let's say a stockbroker and selling them in the market for the current bid price. Later, when the price goes down, they can buy the same number from the market and return them to the broker. The trader need not go through all these steps in practice though and they can simply opt to sell first and buy later, to make a profit from a bearish market.

Hedge Funds, Hedgers, and individuals who are well-versed in technical analysis of candlestick patterns are the chief stock market participants who go for this technique known as "Short trades" or more commonly as "Short Selling." Borrowing may be enabled by your stockbroker or through Securities Borrowing and Lending (SBL) platforms - and the stock or asset borrowed can come from SBL platforms or even from a retailer going long.

Though this process sounds like a piece of cake when explained, there is more to it than meets the eye – and that is the involved risk. The profit of short selling in an intraday trade may be as easy as falling off a log. When you borrow stocks for a period beyond a day, expecting a bearish market, it is a whole other story.

The risk here is that a stock can only drop to zero, no matter what. But when a stock's price begins to skyrocket, there is no knowing the heights to which the event would take it, crushing the short seller under it. The profit of a short sell is limited, but the loss can, unfortunately, be unlimited. So, without a strong analysis of the fundamentals and technical data it can be out-right heedless to go short. Stock market lessons on all platforms and from all sources keep recommending that neither a beginner nor a master trader should disregard the risk-to-reward ratio of a trade before entering one.

This is one of the key points to be grasped as it can open the lock of many possibilities.

What Peculiarity Of The Stock Market Led To This Event?

As we discussed, the expectation that a stock would drop dead soon leads institutional investors to borrow stocks of the company and sell them, creating open positions in the market. But later, they need to buy the open short positions to satisfy the conditions laid forth by the short-interest ratio (or days-to-cover ratio). This is known as "Short covering."

Ideally, short covering is done to reap the profits of short selling; that is, the stocks are bought when the stock price drops as expected. But in case the plan goes south, and the market stock price does not, the short seller would be forced to buy the corresponding stocks for a price higher than the borrowed and sold price. This obligation to cover short positions can cause a lot of panic and can disturb the market.

One of the effects of such situations is a phenomenon known commonly as Short Squeezing. The eventuality known by the term short squeezing was the prime reason behind the stock market anomaly that took place between December 2020 and January 2021, alongside the influence of "Gamma Squeezing." Hence the event is known as the "GameStop Short Squeezing" event of 2021. You will get to know more about short squeezing now.

What Is A Short Squeeze? The Relation Between Short Squeezing Short Positions, And Public Float

Short squeeze, which also goes by the term "Bear Squeeze," is now relatively easier to understand, especially since retailers, institutional investors, and hedgers would jump right in to grab the opportunity to short sell if they sense a bearish market will come to pass shortly.

When a bearish market is predicted wrongly, the short positions created are not solely from the short-selling itself. When the tendency to borrow is on the rise, more and more short positions keep getting created. Let's use a hypothetical situation again to understand this better.

Consider a publicly listed and traded company and let us name it 'LMnO.' The stock market expects it to fall significantly. To keep it simple, let us consider the company has a total public float of 100 shares.

Given the circumstances of the company's fundamentals, trader A borrows all 100 of the stocks and short sells them to trader B. When the news regarding the anticipated dip in the stock is reported, trader C approaches trader B, borrows the stock from them and short sells it to trader D. This chain reaction can continue for several stages, all of which the traders A, B, C, or D may not be aware of.

What has this process affected? These repeated borrowings and shortings have created 200 short positions with traders A and C. Both traders need to buy back 100 stocks each to short cover their positions, while the public float never increases from the initial 100.

The situation not only creates a demand to buy in terms of number but also in terms of the price going up. The price keeps skyrocketing owing to both the news revolving around the squeeze and the buyers holding their positions to go long.

This unexpected price rise is known as Short Squeezing.

As for 'LmnO', it made lemonade with the lemons the fundamental analysts gave it and is all cool now.

So, the Short Squeezing phenomenon and the resultant rise in the stock's (or the asset's) price has nothing to do directly with the company's fundamentals.

Long Squeeze, Future Contracts Squeeze, And Gamma Squeeze

In contrast, the phenomenon known by the term "Long Squeeze" involves the dip in the price of a stock while a bullish market was expected to ensue. The difference is that Short Squeezing involves the possibility of unlimited loss, but Long Squeeze risks are limited by the initial buying price of the stock. Long squeezes are also a lot less probable and less impactful as compared to a short squeeze.

Both short squeeze and long squeeze can happen with future contracts as well, and these events are encompassed under the definition of the term "Future Contracts Squeeze."

Gamma Squeeze, on the other hand, involves Options Trading. This occurs when options market makers are required to hedge their trades on the underlying stocks. The GameStop Short Squeeze occurred partially owing to Gamma squeeze as well.

Usually, the symbol delta is used to indicate the change in the option depending on the price action of the underlying stock. The Delta of an option is the tool with which market makers hedge their calls.

"Gamma" is the term used to express the rate of change of "Delta." The changes in both the delta and the gamma of an option (and thereby of the underlying stock) result in Gamma Squeezing.

A Brief Account Of Some Previous Short Squeeze Events

(i) Panic of 1901:

This was a dramatic and mind-boggling event that developed

over a course of 24 years.

By the beginning of the 1880s, James J. Hill, who held the majority of stocks of the Great Northern Railway, was relentlessly looking for ways to expand the business into Chicago. Meanwhile, E. H. Harriman, the major stakeholder of the Union Pacific Railroad, was also searching for similar business prospects.

Harriman went to the Burlington head, Charles Elliott Perkins, and bought Burlington's shares for the whopping asking price. Then he decided to take control over the Great Northern Railway, to make up for his losses with Burlington.

The venture he began on May 3rd of 1901 came to be known as the "Northern Pacific Corner." However, he was still short on 40,000 stocks, which he could not cover. His plans were sabotaged by Jacob Shiff (his broker).

Hill did his research and found that he could control the company if he could claim more common stocks. So, he tracked down JP Morgan who was out of his office on a holiday at that time, and placed an order for 150,000 common stocks, which Hill knew Morgan had.

Now the game was on between James J. Hill with his partner JP Morgan, who competed over the stocks of the Northern Pacific Railway company with their common rival, EH Harriman. Jacob Shiff was thrown out of the scenario on the 7th of May when the two other parties acquired a total of 94% of the company's shares. All these activities and competition caused the shares of the Northern Pacific Railway to lack shares, but both parties were unwilling to give up.

On the trading day that followed, the spread of this news triggered panic amongst all active stock market participants. The short-selling that followed caused the event known as the Panic of 1901.

Later, Morgan and Hill entered a truce in 1904 under the Supreme

Court of the United States to somewhat settle the events.

By then, both the smaller retail traders and the stocks that were related to this event and the stock were affected drastically. Rumors are that the stock that cost $150 was traded for up to $1000 in May 1901, showing an uncontrollable case of a short squeeze.

(ii) The 2008 Porsche Short Squeeze

The Panic of 1901 was a case of two parties over one stock. The next event to be discussed is a much more recent one, revolving around one magnate and two companies.

Wendelin Wiedeking was CEO of Porsche and a member of the supervisory board of Volkswagen AG in 2008 – both companies listed with the Frankfurt Stock Exchange under the blue-chip stock market index, Xetra DAX.

The mechanical engineer turned businessman attempted to have Porsche take over Volkswagen. The price of Volkswagen AG shares multiplied to about five times its initial price. But the Short Squeeze also left the Volkswagen AG with a debt of about €10 billion.

Wiedeking was charged with market manipulation; nevertheless, he walked away unscathed and with most of the profits to his claim.

(iii) Falcone's MAAX Holdings Short Squeeze

Once a hockey player who sustained an injury and a Harvard Graduate, Philip Falcone had met with all kinds of highs and lows ever since he was a child. In 2012, he came to know that a financial institution was about to short the high-yielding bonds of MAAX Holdings, a Canadian bathroom products manufacturer, and he bought the entire lot. He had then lent some of the bonds and bought them back.

Later when Falcone ceased to lend bonds, the short-sellers could no longer cover their short positions. This was the digital era, unlike 1901, and most of the traders did not divulge the solution. Some sellers figured it out and approached Falcone in person.

By mid-2012, Philip Falcone and his venture Harbinger Capital Partners were under legal action for securities fraud amongst other charges. He fought for about a year, after which he admitted to the charges against him and his company. He paid about $10 million as civil penalties in total.

(iv) Martin Shkreli and his 2015 case

Shkreli was called "Pharma Bro" by the media and often addressed as a "short-seller" – so it was big news if he ever went along with his trades. He was even known to naked short sell.

His areas of interest were mainly the Pharma sector and capital. He founded and co-founded several firms under these niches. Shkreli had at times predicted serious price changes and was the only one who did so, making him a suspect in various frauds. His case may be the most complicated case of a short squeeze and financial frauds, which we may have to discuss under the context.

He is best known for notoriously intervening in the stock prices of a few pharmaceutical stocks – effectively sabotaging their prices. Post-trial, he was convicted to seven years in prison.

(v) The GameStop Short Squeeze of 2020-2021

This will be our main case under discussion. Come on a journey to learn more about the biggest social engineered short squeeze.

What Is The Gravity Of Gamestop Short Squeeze (2020-2021)?

The GameStop short squeeze and gamma squeeze occurred right

after (and in some ways, along with) the 2020 Stock Market Crash owing mostly to the coronavirus pandemic. It was also a small and short-lived victory of the masses in terms of money, volumes, and time. But it was something that had never happened before and no one had expected that something of this nature and magnitude could happen.

As beginners and soon-to-be successful stock market participants, general know-how of such events and understanding the case at hand would help with going down the less-ventured roads like those of squeezes and other stock market anomalies.

CHAPTER III

*The Players of the Game –
GameStop and WallStreetBets*

Now that you are acquainted with the terms and concepts involved in the issue, you have the tools to dissect it. You only need to get to know the entities involved in the short squeeze episode of 2021.

1. Gamestop

GameStop Corp. is the world's largest video game and related merchandise retailer by the sheer number of its retail stores. The company has stores in several countries in the North American, Australian, and European continents as well as New Zealand.

The stores are run by the GameStop Corporation and operate under the brand names of GameStop, EB Games, ThinkGeek, and Micromania-Zing, of which ThinkGeek and GameStop retail stores are more popular to gamers.

The Story Of Gamestop As A Business

GameStop had a relatively humble beginning in contrast to its place on the Fortune 500 list for the past few years. The company was founded in the latter months of 1982 by James B. McCurry and Gary M. Kusin and started functioning from a regional mall in Dallas, Texas. McCurry and Kusin were together at the Harvard Business School where they developed a friendship that made them stand out from their classmates.

The firm was named "Babbage's Inc." after Charles Babbage who envisioned digitally programmable computers for the first time and is the "father of the computer." It was conceived as an educational software retailer and sold computers and related technology for starters.

In February 1983, McCurry and Kusin managed to get Ross Henry Perot (business magnate and politician) to invest in the company, which grew their business. The partners kept experimenting with the kind of products they sold and found what worked best. By the end of 1983, they opened four more of their stores in Dallas, marking their growth as a chain store giant.

In 1984, they acquired Software Etc. and re-launched as Babbage's Etc. LLC. They began selling video games for Atari 2600 which was a big hit back then. They took up Nintendo games too in three years. Nintendo was on the rise back then, owing to the newfound market for the Pokémon franchise games.

The partners completed all procedures to go public in the following years, from 1988 to 1991. By then, the larger share of their profits found its way into the company's accounts through video games.

The company's next big association was in 1994 when they revamped themselves by merging the independent subsidiaries of Babbage's and Software Inc. to form the NeoStar Retail Group, Inc. In 1995, the then Software Etc. chairman Leonard Riggio bought the chains and was reappointed as the chairman of NeoStar's executive committee. The name Neostar may have been influenced by the "Matrix" movie franchise protagonist "Neo" that was a major box office success and trendy at the time. Gary Kusin resigned from the company the same year.

The company had not expected they would be required to file Chapter 11 bankruptcy because they could not amass the credit necessary for the holiday season's hectic business. Although McCurry had become the Chairman and CEO of the NeoStar Retail group during the remodeling, he had to step down as Chief executive and President because of this move. Thomas G. Plaskett entered the scene as a board member.

In 1999, a hodge-podge of developments led Leonard Riggio's Barnes & Noble Electronics firm to acquire Funco, Inc. The price paid for the company is said to have been a whopping 215 million USD.

Funco Inc. was already running a successful video game retail chain operating in over 400 strip malls under the name "Funco-Land." The two firms, Funco Inc. and NeoStar Retail Group (or Barnes & Noble or Babbage's Inc., as you would like to call it) are merged under Riggio and Plaskett to be renamed as "GameStop Inc.," as we know it today.

GameStop's unique business model included the buy-sell-trade program, which they follow to this day. Riggio also conceived and launched the e-commerce website dedicated to video games, tech, and merchandise – gamestop.com – parallel to the strip mall chain stores, further expanding the reach and scope of the venture.

The company was taken to new heights when it was incorporated as GameStop Corp. and began its steps toward its Initial Public Offering (IPO). In the meantime, Riggio was also busy acquiring the rights of a gaming magazine "Game Informer" after its launch in 1991, in hopes of better outreach and endorsement of the brand. He had also not dissolved the parent company, Barnes & Noble; instead, he reshaped it as Barnes & Noble Booksellers.

GameStop Corp. was successfully taken public in 2002 and

was listed under the ever-prestigious New York Stock Exchange (NYSE) under the stock symbol of "GME." Sixty-seven percent of the stakes were still held under the power of Barnes & Noble until 2004.

In 2004, 59 percent of the shares of GameStop were spread thinner under Barnes & Noble stakeholders. Thus, GameStop has been a completely independent corporate company since 2004.

Starting from 2004, GameStop saw a stage of expansion when it acquired Electronics Boutique Games (EB Games), Rhino Video Games from Blockbuster, Micromania, the Norwegian stores of Free Record Shop, Kongregate, Spawn Labs, BuyMyTronics, Impulse, Simply Mac, Spring Mobile, and many other companies that could complement them. Thus, GameStop expanded itself from the United States of America's grounds into Canada, New Zealand, Australia, and Europe by 2016.

GameStop had also introduced innovative perks, rewards, and customer loyalty programs in 2010, which made more gamers walk into the stores in herds.

Though GameStop survived the hedge fund triggered short squeeze and financial crisis of 2008, things turned unfavorable in 2016. More and more video game sellers developed competent online commercial platforms, while GameStop's captain seemed asleep at the wheel. Its online platform, though it was one of the pioneers in the niche and genre, unfortunately fell behind. 2016 also saw a 16 percent drop in both GameStop sales and the stock price of GME.

As if that loss was not enough, some former sales employees revealed that the program called "Circle of Life" by GameStop had them lying to customers. They revealed in February 2017 that they were forced to urge gamers to trade games with them but paid practically nothing for them.

GameStop patched this mistake up abruptly the same month

but was not saved. Reports, interviews, testaments, social media memes, and all sorts of content mushroomed up against Game-Stop's behavior towards both their employees and their customers. This trend continued up until the 2021 short squeeze and has not ceased even then. Some news reports and social media content even seem to express joy in reporting whenever GameStop decides to shut down some of their stores or if a major employee resigns.

The CEO of GameStop in 2018, Michael Mauler, resigned for personal reasons; it was rumored that he left the company after disagreeing with potential fraud.

Gamestop Entered The Esports Arena In 2019.

Though GameStop kept spreading positive news, agencies including Reuters reported that GameStop was looking for buyers and that they needed a buyout of shares to cope with their financial situation.

GameStop further tarnished itself in 2020, by keeping stores open despite the COVID-19 pandemic and forced the employees to turn up to work. The official social media accounts of Game-Stop were also seen making snarky comments. Even when they dealt with unfortunate and rare occurrences of customers misbehaving towards employees, the company took the less graceful route.

Just when GameStop was recovering its reputation after about half a decade of a bad game, the social media-driven short squeeze occurred, hyping it again in the media.

Ventures Under The Gamestop Umbrella

Although the digital era shut the business for many retail chains that sell electronics and other goods, GameStop retail stores held on in the field. GameStop is also one of the very few retail stores that urge the consumer communities to trade games (in good, re-usable, and reasonable condition) for either cash or store (chain) credit; making their popularity spread wider. The social media cries out loud repeatedly about how little most GameStop retail stores and their employees are ready to pay for decent games – even the rare ones.

GameStop Inc. is also the proprietor of the gaming magazine "Game Informer" published on a five-week frequency. The publication presents the gaming community members with all sorts of perks that come with the subscriptions that can be bought from their retail stores. With the advent of newer and better video games that are developed to compete with online games and apps, the chain flourished.

GameStop's business also involves buying used games and re-usable accessories. These transactions accounted for 44% of their gross profit from just 25% of the total sales in the year 2013 – there is no arguing they knew the used game industry. The stores also offer a bonus for gamers who place orders in advance. The rewards can include everything from in-game features or sound-tracks to merchandise like artbooks, plushies, figurines, posters, and T-shirts – all depending on the brand and version of the game ordered.

The consumers, gamers in this case, can keep themselves updated about upcoming releases, offers, exclusive developer interviews, product information and demos, etc. whenever they visit the store. The in-store television network has been introduced solely for this purpose. "GameStop TV" was a revolutionary endeavor at the time of its conception. The content is updated either once every month or at least every five weeks.

When the movie DVD market flourished, GameStop leaped right in at the opportunity and launched "MovieStop" - a movie and merchandise chain dedicated to both new and traded-in owned movies. The chain took an unfortunate turn and was sold to another business and was later shut down in 2016.

When internet gaming platforms became more widespread and gamers found their haven online, GameStop Inc. bought Impulse and renamed it "GameStop PC," better known as "GameStop PC Downloads." The business claims to offer downloads of over 1500 cataloged PC games - mostly for free.

The Video Game Industry Is Leaving Gamestop Behind

As video game usage is surging to record highs, brick-and-mortar retail chains like GameStop are left behind. Gamers nowadays can download and stream games to their PCs and consoles, which is one of the reasons why many gamers prefer to purchase online instead of buying physical discs in-person.

Trips these days to physical stores are not necessary anymore as consumption habits change and the digital world flourishes and evolves. However, GameStop still relies on physical scales despite the reality that e-commerce platforms are taking off.

As more people transition to digital transactions, the less revenue and profits GameStop makes year after year. Other people also noticed that GameStop stocks were undervalued, which made them want to do something to help. Redditors from the WallStreetBets group decided to increase its value "to the moon" by buying its stocks to get back at the hedge funds who were taking advantage and profiting off businesses that are declining. This resulted in a "short squeeze" and hedge funds like Melvin Capital that had shorted its stocks had to buy more shares to cover their massive losses.

As this phenomenon gained global attention, GameStop stocks soared more than 12,000 in January 2021 which is incredibly larger than its $4 value around the same time a year ago.

The stock's price has since then swung back and forth after it reached its all-time-high value after Robinhood and other stock-trading platforms blocked the ability of investors to buy Game-Stop and other heavily shorted stocks.

2. Robinhood – The App Until January 2021

The Robinhood trading app is a retail platform that offers Investment and Trading, free of commission, in stocks, different exchange-traded funds (ETFs), and Options. Through Robinhood Crypto, you can also buy and sell cryptocurrencies like Bitcoin (BTC), Ethereum (ETH), Litecoin (LTC), and Dogecoin (DOGE).

The app also offers short introductions to the financial markets, investments, and trades for beginners. Furthermore, the platform comes with a competitive interest Cash Management feature that enables them to pay interest for your uninvested cash. Robinhood does this by directing the users' unused funds to their partner banks. Robinhood Financial LLC and Robinhood Crypto, LLC are fully owned subsidiaries of Robinhood Markets, Inc.

The official website clearly states where revenue comes from. Robinhood Financial LLC emphasizes for transparency, and the sources may be classified into three main streams: (i) interest earned from the cash balances in customers' accounts, (ii) payment for selling order flow information (corresponds to high-frequency trades (HFT) mostly carried out by proficient algorithm-based traders and not the regular retail traders' portfolios), and (iii) lending margins for trades.

The History And Credibility Of Robinhood

Robinhood had a knack for High-Frequency Trading and knew the heart of traders (of all shapes and sizes) right from its birth seven years ago.

Vladimir Tenev and Baiju Bhatt, the two founders of the financial service firm under the title Robinhood, were also the developers of customized high-frequency algorithm trading software for a surprising number of financial institutions (mostly hedge fund companies) of New York City. They were thus practically a (latent and covert) part of the New York city's conglomerate circles, and hence insiders of Wall Street itself.

Tenev and Bhatt's claims seem to say that they envisioned the platform as a Moses for the common man - the New York Stock Exchange and financial independence being the Promised Land - because they knew the financial market's dunes and sands and the oases and mirages so well. They say the company's name, for instance, comes from its mission to "provide everyone with access to the financial markets, (and) not just the wealthy." As per reports, the founders have openly stated that most brokerage firms charged the traders 50 to 100 times the actual cost of the trading process.

The co-founders Bhatt and Tenev met as master's degree classmates at Stanford University and were roommates. Tenev dropped out of his Ph.D. from Stanford to go to New York with Bhatt and by 2010 they developed an HFT algorithm-trading company that went by the name "Celeris." The firm was dissolved the same year and "Chronos Research" was founded.

Through this firm, the then 23-year-olds sold low-latency software to other trading firms, hedge funds, and banks.

Also through the experiences in this firm, Bhatt and Tenev realized that Wall Street giants did not need to pay much of a penny to go about doing their business, and that at the same time, most retail investors were charged hefty fees for their trades, no matter what kind. This realization is how they ended up conceiving a Robinhood for everyone.

Robinhood was launched in 2013 and after going public in 2015, the app was used mostly by millennials. Tenev and Bhatt were almost of the same age group. They executed the orders placed with them indirectly through market makers and trading venues who offered them rebates through "payment for order flow" practices.

Growth, Room For Improvement, And Openness To Constructive Criticism

Robinhood only saw growth for many years after its birth. Within three years of launching, Robinhood may have been the only broker that had shown such remarkable growth. According to Wikipedia, "As of May 2018, Robinhood raised a total of $539 million in venture capital funding, with the last valuation at $5.6 billion, up from their previous valuation of $1.3 billion."

This growth may have been a consequence of two of their moves:

(i) Robinhood stepped into Commission-free Cryptocurrency Trading - Robinhood became a cryptocurrency trader through their Robinhood Crypto, LLC venture by the end of January 2018. For starters, Robinhood Crypto offered their customers options for buying and selling Bitcoin (BTC) and Ethereum (ETH), and started offering Litecoin (LTC) and Dogecoin (DOGE) soon enough after. Users from California, Massachusetts, Missouri, Montana, Wisconsin, and New Mexico were the first to trade bitcoins with Robinhood Crypto. This venture furthered their popularity amongst the masses of all generation demographics.

(ii) Robinhood announced that they would step into banking by the end of the year and had already made proceedings for a United States Banking License. As promised, this feature was up and active by 2019. Robinhood offers, ever since, checking and savings accounts with debit cards issued by the Sutton Bank based in Ohio.

But growth neither meant that they had zero room for improvement, nor that Robinhood's leadership team was not open to constructive criticism. They remained responsive to customer feedback, the responses of the masses, ever-changing trends, news, and potential negative publicity.

Robinhood took prompt action to respond to the security breach of July 2019 and outages resulting from a leap year handling coding error in March of 2020.

When the news of a millennial's suicide and his account that had a negative balance of $730,000 was spread, Robinhood promptly responded by investigating the case and making amends to its platform's norms. This occurred in June 2020.

August 2020

By August 2020, Robinhood made new venture funding round raising $200 million and a valuation of $11.2 billion. Robinhood was rumored to hit IPO as Vladimir Tenev and Baiju Bhatt had envisioned back in 2013.

Also, many new traders who hit the market after having lost day jobs due to the coronavirus pandemic had opted for Robinhood as their go-to trading platform.

Late 2020 And Early 2021

Though the August 2020 funding was a big surprise amid the COVID-19 induced financial crisis, the GameStop Short Squeeze of 2021 pushed the limits. Robinhood raised many more funds, and a colossal $3.4 billion was a number that kept popping up by the end of January 2021.

This event raised the biggest questions against Robinhood ever.

Mixed Opinions

When the 2021 GameStop Short Squeeze happened, the public had mixed opinions regarding Robinhood.

Everyone started blaming Robinhood and Citadel for the trade restrictions that didn't allow to buy more GameStop stocks. After weeks after the GameStop Short Squeeze event (some media as late as mid-February 2021). Some vigilant observers believed it was clear that Citadel and Robinhood could both be suspected of having a larger role than was obvious in the event - whether the allegation is true or not needed to be investigated.

3. Wallstreetbets Reddit Group

The Reddit WallStreetBets community was founded on January 31st, 2012. The group is also referred to as WSB. Even before the 2021 short squeeze, WallStreetBets was famous for its venturesome trade choices that mostly and frequently involved shorting, options trading, and other risky, rocky roads. They are also commended for their "colorful" jargons or "lingo." The community is also expressed by the alternative spellings of "r/WallStreetBets" and "Wallstreetbets," interchangeably.

The members of Wallstreetbets may be individuals, groups, or small financial firms who are all interested in discussing the New York Stock Market, Wall Street, the inside games, stocks, options, futures, and everything related to the stock market.

Wallstreetbets are best known for the 2021 short squeeze event, where they took down many hedge funds through an extra-dramatic turn of events using GameStop (GME) stock and its options as their medium of choice.

The next chapter will discuss the length of the event but first, let's talk about the community's founder and short history.

Wsb's Founder And Brief History

Jaime Rogozinski, the author of "WallStreetBets: How Boomers Made the World's Biggest Casino for Millennials," founded the r/WallStreetsBets Reddit in 2012 while he was working as an IT consultant in Washington, DC. The reason he started WSB was that he was told by his fellow investors in other forums that his investing ideas were too risky and would not work out. He decided to create a subreddit because he wanted a safe community where people could talk about high-risk trades in an unapologetic way while gaining short-term money with disposable income.

During their early years, WSB was still trying to establish its identity but some members organized events and met from time to time. From 2013-2016, the Reddit group remained small and the amount of subscribers didn't hit 100,000 subscribers until 2017.

The WallStreetBets community had played an important role in democratizing the investing world as it grew even more in 2019 when Charles Schwab Corp and Fidelity Investment eliminated and abolished commissions on trading. What was once exclusive to only the big Wall Street players suddenly became accessible to common traders.

The following year, the sub had grown to over a million subscribers and was full of newbie traders sharing the different ups and downs in their journey. Unfortunately, WallStreetBets is no longer what it once was nor how Jamie envisioned it to be. He was eventually kicked out of the community he started in April 2020 after collective attempts of other moderators.

By February 2021, r/WallStreetBets was quickly booming as it reached more than 8 million members. The gamification of trading is indeed on the rise, but for many, the GameStop fiasco might be the first time they've heard about the community. Some people wanted to join out of curiosity, while others wanted to join and become part of a movement because they were aware of the impact of the collective buying power of retail traders in capital markets.

As the fiasco was still playing out, Rogozinski has reportedly sold the rights to his life story to Brett Ratner and RatPac Entertainment. According to his producers, his story will be told in the form of a movie first before venturing into other mediums.

CHAPTER IV

The 2021 GameStop Short Squeeze Explained" or "The 2021 GameStop Short Squeeze Debunked

The revolutionary events that took place in the New York Stock Market in the last months of 2020 and into 2021 may be the most unprecedented in this arena. Nothing of this magnitude had ever happened before, nor was it expected in any way.

The best of financial market experts had not even theorized something of this nature or magnitude may have happened. The biggest irony may be that this event took place in the world's most observed, participated, and secured market, while the triggers and catalysts for the events were completely public and anyone could have seen them.

We could not blame anyone for not having anticipated the dimension of what was coming, because the whales, sharks, and wolves of Wall Street were all under the impression that a social media horde could never upset the apple cart they had always held dear, and above all, as their very own!

This was an event where the "very average unwashed joes in the street" momentarily beat the institutional investors and hedge funds, while also again putting into controversy a company that had always underpriced the customers' goods and overpriced their own for decades..

This incident happened in a very modernly apt way – through social media and through thousands of people who did not even know each other. A herd mentality kind of situation took matters from the unexpected to levels far beyond belief.

2021 Gamestop Short Squeeze - From A To Z

We have seen from the different phases of GameStop as a company. GameStop hit the lowest rock bottom with the advent of online games, growth of e-commerce for gaming, and more people advancing towards making fancy personal collections from old games for themselves. GameStop's history almost stopped with online games and the company was going to lay in ruin.

Institutional investors, particularly hedge funds, were also under the impression that the company was going broke. As per their fundamental analysis, technical analysis, market news, and experience, they began selling the stocks, in hope of handsome profits by short-selling; then, they waited.

Wallstreetbets Enter The Scene.

WallStreeBets was one of the many subreddits - a sub-forum within the social media platform Reddit that was meant for people to discuss the financial markets, especially the NYSE and the stocks and derivatives traded within them. They also discussed personal financial moves, NYSE events, world markets, Wall Street, and almost everything that came under the definition of finance and economics.

One of the members who uses a profile under the name "deepF---ingvalue" posted in the group that they had $50000 on hand and that they had decided to invest in the GameStop GME stock. This (seemingly) random stock selection announcement was made in September 2019. The member said that they entered a call option for the 50000 dollars - just for the sake of fun!

The user was naturally scoffed and laughed at for entering long, a stock that was dropping so badly. The user was called many things - a liar, a fraud, a Benami of GameStop, a fool, a show-off, among many other things.

And as a matter of course, they kept losing a lot of their money as the stock kept dropping and dropping; however, the user kept updating the group with whatever was happening.

This drop in stock prices also triggered a discussion within the group. For some reason (or the lack of it) the matter became viral and trending on not just Reddit, but almost all social media platforms where sharing was a norm.

Given the CoViD-19 situations, the business that was based on retail stores, for the most part, was naturally having a hard time keeping their finances rolling. The company had no hope by June 2020, though its online stores were having a slightly better movement.

The Bigger Players

The shocking twist happened in August 2020, when GameStop entered into a multi-strategic partnership agreement with none other than Microsoft. The same month Chewy, a subsidiary of PetSmart that was funded by institutional investors like BC Partners Advisors LP and Morgan Stanley Financial Services Company, was reported to have bought 9% of the shares of GameStop.

The billionaire entrepreneurship declared that they were joining GameStop to bring about massive changes to the online space and to expand it as an online conglomerate. While some Redditers grew skeptical, many others branded them all fools.

The Power Of Reading

The doubting Thomases, of course, did some serious digging in the right direction and got their hands on the public data all hedge funds need to publish that states their transactions. By putting together all the public data, they found out with a bit of brainstorming that hedge funds and institutional investors had not only been shorting on GME but also that they had shorted about 138% of the public float!

GameStop short position numbers were a surprising and tremendous turn of events for the other traders. No one could remember a time when there was such a big number of open short positions in recent history (or lore). GameStop GME was at the time, the stock with the biggest number of short positions open on NYSE.

This news not only took Redditers by surprise but also got them curious. So many of the members on the WallStreetBets subreddit forum decided to buy more of the stock to simply make use of the opportunity (as much as they could with their funds) when the shorters would try to cover their shorts. Redditors got busy soon after, but they only comprised a relatively small number.

This decision and discussions got a huge hype on social media. Everyone was suddenly more interested in the viral stock. More and more retail traders learned about the event and began buying the stock, but no one sold them except the hedge funds and institutional investors who either were unaware of the developments or at least underestimated the power of the commoners.

The relentless GameStop "buy spree" took the stock from the price of around $4 to something around $450. As for "deepF---ckingvalue", they reported that their $50,000 stocks were now worth an eye-popping $25 million. They had also booked profits several times by then.

This skyrocketing in the price of GameStop stock was remarkable. The event - or the price-hike - was not at all based on any fundamental analysis, which is usually Wall Street's Hedgefund strong game. Institutional investors and hedge funds were soon seen eating dust from the unorganized bull strikes. They had no choice but to short cover, but no one was selling the stocks.

Some even reported that the big whales of Wall Street even set out (out of their usual "eat 'em all" way) in search of a solution. Social media platforms were overflowing with discussions, memes, and campaigns.

The case, of course, is an anomaly - some people prefer to believe that something might have gone gravely wrong for something so unusual to have happened.

However, the event has two causes: (i) institutional investors got too acquisitive to stop before the short position percentages got too out of hand, and (ii) the traders on the Reddit group WallStreetBets made the right move promptly and on time. The situation could easily have otherwise been manipulated by the sharks for yet another case of classic pump and dump.

Social Media Responses

Social media soon took a shine to the event. The story of commoners who seized the day and stopped the game of sharks took over public platforms by large. The public went to bat for their representatives through their responses. The world seemed to be batting for the people who grabbed the opportunity to give the financial investors around the world a taste of their own medicine.

Gamers and traders who were acquainted with the GameStop chain and company through the decades commended how well their slogan "Power to the Players" eventually achieved a new (or rather, real) meaning. Redditors even mocked the stock exchanges' capitalist tendencies by saying that they "used capitalism to destroy capitalism."

One could not blame the common man for such comments. They could never forget the insults hedge funds added to their injuries on several occasions (stock market crashes, economic crises, pump and dump, frauds, etc.), especially the ones from back in 2008.

Hedge funds, authorities, institutional investors, stock exchanges, and even authorities never wasted any opportunity they had to blame the common people's lack of knowledge in financial matters. Even when inflations and stock market crashes were caused by their trading methods and rivalry.

Be it student loans, credit cards, debt, or even the 2008 stock market crash, the Wall Street mafia blamed the public's lack of budgeting. They had always silenced the protests that demanded rules and regulations (that many nations had very successfully and effectively implemented on their stock exchanges) to prevent such events from happening. They backed themselves and their gluttonous actions by saying that the market was open for all – sometimes in the line of challenging them outright.

The truth is that the public neither ever lacked the knowledge, nor the wit – they were just not a part of Wall Street – and Wall Street was in for a big unpleasant surprise. They teamed up initially with no intention of taking down anyone – they were simply part of a discussion.

What happened later, that is the process that took down many hedgers, just 'happened!' The participants were all up for the game mostly out of sheer curiosity. Most of them had lost many of their elements of financial security, while a minority had practically nothing much to lose – all as an effect of the global pandemic and the financial crash that followed. Not many even had their jobs or insurances at stake –they practically vented out their rage from all these years.

Given the opportunity, they all started buying the GameStop stock against the bearish market without second thoughts. Many of them plunged right in with all of what little was left from their savings. The investor giants made the mistake of laughing at this and held their ground, while the small fish were practically dragging some of the earth from under their feet.

This short squeeze inflicted by the masses is truly one of a kind because never had a party other than the hedgers ever created one.

The institutions had no room left to short cover once the mob began shaking their earth more publicly. Now that the public they have always mocked and underestimated had outnumbered them – not by their financial weightage, of course, but by their effectiveness as a mob – and had started making profits from the same loopholes they were making money from all this time, the institutional investors and hedge funds suddenly started requiring rules and regulations upon the financial markets to prevent such phenomena. They were influencing all possible agencies, brokers, and other institutions to somehow bring down the impact the tiny bulls were collectively venting on their bear-bent backs.

Robinhood And The Questions That Should Have Been Asked Earlier.

Robinhood was one of the very few low-fee brokers that facilitated the traders with the opportunity to buy GameStop stocks when the buy order surges hit the market's counters.

By the end of January, Robinhood, unexpectedly and out of their way, bailed. Traders could no longer buy any shares of 13 companies at the risk of a short squeeze, including GME stocks.

This move caused a larger uproar than ever. The public believed that this change may be a part of the influence of Wall Street money.

Robinhood co-founder Vlad Tenev soon spoke online on why they had to back out. Tenev, on behalf of his company and the company's correspondences, stated that this move was purely to meet the "many financial requirements, including SEC net capital obligations and clearinghouse deposits." They say, "Some of these requirements fluctuate based on volatility in the markets and can be substantial in the current environment".

What would the public understand from that statement? That Robinhood was saving the Wall Street business model.

The fact that Robinhood was no longer letting anyone (only the smaller traders who were trading using them) buy, but were letting them sell was enough for most of the participants to realize the threat, which in the most basic terms would say that "you can either sell your stocks enabling the sharks short cover or be at the risk of holding your stakes for as long as you want, no matter where the prices go thereafter."

Did Robinhood Descend From The Fortress Of "Citadel"?

Despite everything, some keener eyes discovered by the first weeks of February 2021 some clues that indicate that the Game-Stop shorting Hedge fund "Citadel" may be the parent of Robinhood.

If this realization is true, then we have no choice but to agree with some websites that state:

"Market Manipulation. Period."

CHAPTER V

2008 Financial Crisis

The 2008 crash created a seismic shock and pushed the world's banking system towards the edge of collapse. The event started when one of the biggest Wall Street investment banks (Lehman Brothers) went bankrupt on September 15, 2008. However, this meltdown had long roots and only became apparent to the world when Lehman Brothers filed for bankruptcy.

The financial system had been in jeopardy for quite some time before this financial shock rattled the industry. Bear Stearns (a US investment bank) had been rescued in March and even Northern Rock (UK mortgage lender) had experienced a run as early as the autumn of 2007.

This incident was considered the greatest shakeup to the global financial system in the last century and its effects devastated many people and caused a systematic loss of trust among financiers. An Anglo-American debt-deflationary was also predicted or anticipated by UK-based author and economist Ann Pettifor in 2003. This projection was followed by her book called "The Coming First World Debt Crisis" in 2006 which became a bestseller after the global financial crisis.

Bankers in the US at that time were making a living out of buying the US mortgages of Americans with a subprime credit score, packaging them with higher-quality mortgages, and selling them as mortgage-backed securities (essentially risk-free assets). However, many homeowners started to default once the US central bank raised interest rates in 2006. These defaults caused housing prices to fall and people found how risky these securities were and how much losses that could happen in this system.

Due to these losses, banks started lending to other institutions with high-interest rates who they assume might be experiencing unrecognized losses. This move was known as the "credit crunch" phase and is what happened to Lehman Brothers. Sadly, this phase eventually got out of control and morphed into something chaotic where everyone stopped lending.

Despite what happened, the dodgy American mortgages themselves were not entirely the root cause of this crisis. The occasion only revealed the staggering vulnerability of the global system as the size of the market was around $1.3 million, and the total was $242 million during its peak in 2007.

The Causes And Their Aftermath

The Independent Financial Crisis Inquiry Commission claimed that the system was so weak and fragile due to a combination of historic regulation of finance caused by politicians, as well as the reckless behavior of materialistic and unprofessional bank executives. Others have identified that corruption is also one of the factors that caused deregulation in the financial industry.

There's no denying that the consequences of this crisis were intense. The fallout caused international trade and industrial production to fall at a faster rate than during the 1930s. A massive number of people lost their jobs and living standards were damaged to a big extent as the global economy went into recession. On the other hand, if we look at the similarities to the 1929 stock market crash, both crises involved so much asset market debt, reckless speculation, and loose credit. In this regard, it's not surprising that this incident was said to be even worse than more than 120 banking crises that happened between 1970 and 2007 (due to bad lending) according to the International Monetary Fund.

Even though trillions of dollars' worth of taxpayer funds and guarantees had prevented this crisis from being as socially destructive as the Great Depression, the harsh reality is that its aftermath was not easy to escape. When we look at historic standards, the global economic recovery had been incredibly weak in many Western countries over the next decade. Andy Haldane, the chief economist of the Bank of England, even estimated in 2010 that the total cost of the financial crash was between $60 trillion and $200 trillion, or between one and five times the planet's GDP.

After this crisis happened more than a decade ago, the global financial system has been enhanced to a certain degree and regulators are now imposing higher liquidity requirements on banks. This event has forced them to increase their capital buffers to monitor the system more closely this time around. Also, banks nowadays are bigger today than they were a decade ago and this growth would not have been possible without the mergers of this crisis.

History Of Hedge Funds

Alfred Winslow Jones, also known as the "Father of the Modern Hedge Fund," created the first hedge fund strategy in 1949 even though this idea had already been explored by investors in the 1920s. He was born in Melbourne, Australia in 1901 to American parents who moved back to the U.S. when he was still a child. He earned his bachelor's degree from Harvard in 1923 before serving as a diplomat in Berlin, Germany. After some time, he decided to study at Columbia University to earn his Ph.D. in Sociology.

After earning his Ph.D., he started working at Fortune magazine as one of their editorial staff. One fateful day in 1948, he was asked by his superiors to write an article about the current investment trends. Little did he know that his life was about to change because of this assignment. He then decided to pursue his idea to become a money manager by investing $40,000 of his own money, and soliciting $60,000, or also known as "leveraging" (borrowing money to buy assets).

By 1952, Jones decided to change the structure of his investment vehicle by giving his managing partners a 20% incentive from his profits, as well as changing their partnerships from general to limited. This investment model remains the template for hedge funds to a large extent.

Back in the 1940s, most people believed that the market was efficient and that sellers could sell stocks at a price point they wanted without any haggling-requests from buyers, an action called "Perfect liquidity." This method was the reason why prices at that time were random and there were no repeated patterns. Anyone who tried to speculate prices was bound to fail.

Jones decided to separate the two stock investment risks by creating a market-neutral portfolio. He knew that these risks had to do with changing stock prices because of the market influence and specific equities that were created by factors individual to that stock.

The Rise And Fall Of Hedge Funds

The 1960S-1970S

More than a decade passed before Alfred Jones' idea took off again.

A Fortune magazine article published in 1966 highlighted how Jones outperformed every mutual fund in the last five years by double-digit figures (even when fees were considered). The huge profits made investors and money managers take notice again and 140 hedge funds were in operation two years later.

The hedge fund industry boomed in the 1960s and by 1969, the first fund of hedge funds was created that gave investors access to other hedge funds through one investment vehicle. However, the stock market crashes of 1969-1970 & 1973-1974 affected its growth and many hedge funds had no other choice but to close as they struggled against market risks. The other hedge funds that were still operating, on the other hand, resorted to even riskier strategies and decided not to follow the original strategy of Jones to get the long-term leverage that they wanted.

Due to the stock market crashes, hedge funds took a while to find themselves in the spotlight again.

The 1980S

In 1980, a guy named Julian Robertson started the Tiger Fund with $8 million in capital. Six years later, an article about him was published regarding his double-digit success which made people want to invest in hedge funds again. Seven years after that article came out, he was estimated to have made $300 million, and during the late '90s his fund was worth over $22 billion.

Robertson's success had ignited the interest of many investors around the world which caused hedge funds to evolve again in the late 1980s. He was known for his mandate of finding the 200 best companies in the world and investing in them and finding the 200 worst companies in the world and going short on them. He also believed that people should probably be in another business if the 200 best didn't do better than the 200 worst companies.

Despite Tiger Funds' collapse in the early 2000s, its legacy still lives on in the industry today as some of its employees back in the day had launched their very own hedge funds which are part of a group of hedge funds known as "Tiger Cubs."

The 1990S

The 1990s was the time when many new hedge funds were formed and a huge outflow of people from the mutual fund industry transferred to the hedge fund industry to enjoy its flexibility and remuneration.

One of the most popular success stories was the high-profile success of George Soros and Jim Rogers' Quantum Fund, also known as the trade that forced the exit of the UK from the European Exchange Rate Mechanism. Just like Tiger Fund, Quantum Fund suffered great losses similar to other hedge funds during the market crashes of the previous decades.

A lot of things happened after the Quantum Fund loss, which affected and shaped the way hedge funds operate. After the 2000 dot-com crash and the global housing crisis of 2008, regulators had brought major changes in hedge fund operations. For example, hedge fund managers and sponsors were now required to register as investment advisors. They also had to submit more requirements, create their code of ethics, update their compliance and operational frameworks, hire additional people like compliance officers, etc. These barriers paved the way for competition to flourish since the hedge fund sector became more institutionalized and professionalized.

Hedge Funds Today

Hedge funds today are quite different from their 1940s and even their 1980s counterparts. The people involved used a far greater variety of strategies and some of them may not use traditional hedging techniques by Jones any longer.

Although the industry had its fair share of ups and downs, they still managed to deliver their best performance in 2020 after more than a decade as their assets rose to $3.6 trillion after an additional $290 billion from October to December 2020. However, the addition of the WSB Redditors into the mix might just completely change the game of what's to come for this industry.

Hedge Fund Characteristics And Requirements

Hedge funds work by pooling funds for investment purposes. They employ a variety of strategies to maximize investor returns and eliminate risk, but they aren't usually subjected to some federal rules and could operate with little or no regulation from the Securities and Exchange Commission (SEC).

Some don't even reveal their strategies, and their fund investments are not transparent. When compared to heavily regulated mutual funds, they are more expensive and the only codes and regulations they have in common are related to fraud and fiduciary duties, which makes it riskier to invest in them compared to other investment options out there.

Also, not everyone who wants to invest could be given a chance as there are certain income, net worth, and other requirements that need to be met to ensure that investors can bear massive losses if such losses occur. Here are some of the requirements:

For people

- Personal income should be $200,000+ per year.
- If married, spouses' combined income should be $300,000+ per year and should be maintained for at least 2 consecutive years.
- Personal net worth should be $1+ million or more.

For entities:

- It can be a trust with $5+ million net worth and should not be formed just to make investments.
- Must have a "sophisticated investor" or a person with experience and knowledge in investing.
- All its equity investors must be accredited investors on their merit.

Fees And Costs

Hedge fund managers are compensated no matter how the fund performs. They usually charge a 1% to 2% investment fee on assets and receive a 20% incentive on profits. The downside is that some hedge funds do not profit because of asset management fees and exchange fees for their fund managers, and investment banks, respectively.

Aside from that, they must pay for any losses to investors first before the manager can take 20%. This incentive structure is known as "Funds high watermark." For instance, if a fund loses 10% in its first year and gains 30% the next year, the manager cannot take the profits from the second year until the 10% loss during the first year was recouped.

When it comes to money withdrawal, some hedge funds can't just withdraw whenever they want. Some managers require a minimum amount and insist on a lock-up or a specified period (around 1-5 years) before investors can withdraw.

Hedge Fund Strategies

To protect hedge funds against the movements of market stocks or securities, they apply different strategies to gain profits without spending their entire budget. Here are some of the strategies:

Long/Short Equity Strategy

The long/short strategy is one of the most famous hedge funds investing methods where an investment manager will purchase undervalued stocks and sell overvalued stocks. 70% are usually invested in long positions, while 30% are invested in more tactical shorting positions. This type of strategy employs a wide variety of techniques in terms of exposure, leverage, holding period, concentrations of market capitalization, and valuation.

Market Neutral Strategy

This hedge fund strategy has a lower risk than the low/short equity strategy because hedge fund managers deploy and target zero net-market exposure that are holding both long and short positions. However, the profits are usually lower since shorts and longs have equal market value. This method is used if investment managers want to reduce the market volatility impact on a fund's performance.

Merger Arbitrage Strategy

This hedge fund strategy looks at the involved risks such as the probability of deals not being completed or closed on time. A merger will then purchase stocks before the acquisition.

Convertible Arbitrage

This hedge fund strategy thrives on volatility and typically goes through multiple steps to be implemented. It involves a long position on bonds (buy) and short positions (sell) on common stock or shares.

Even though there are certain risks associated with this strategy, investment managers usually capitalize on mispricing inefficiencies and errors between a convertible bond and its underlying stock. For instance, if an undervalued convertible bond is cheap to its underlying stock, the arbitrageur should take a long position in the convertible bond and a short part in the stock. On the other hand, if a convertible bond is overpriced, the arbitrageur should take a short position in the convertible bond and a long position instead.

Capital Structure Arbitrage

The objective of this hedge fund strategy is to profit from the issuing company's capital pricing structure inefficiencies. This strategy is used when investment managers prefer to go long in one security while going short in another security at the same time, leading to profits regardless of the overall market direction.

Fixed-Income Arbitrage

The objective of this hedge fund strategy is to gain profits on small price inconsistencies. This is done when investment managers oppose long and short positions taken in a swap and a treasury bond, like in a swap-spread arbitrage (the most common type of fixed-income arbitrage). The profits from this strategy type are relatively low though and there's a potential to incur heavy losses, which is the reason why this strategy is referred to as 'Picking up nickels in front of a steamroller!'

Event-Driven

The investment decisions in this hedge fund strategy are triggered by specific events such as bankruptcies, asset sales, shareholder buybacks, debt exchanges, security issuance mergers or takeover, and other capital structure adjustments.

Global Macro

Investment managers who use this highly leveraged hedge fund strategy focus on investments not just in a variety of bonds and stocks, but also commodities, options, derivatives, and currencies. They capitalize on market trends (either upward or downward), asset classes, and financial instruments through macroeconomic indicators analysis and investment thesis development. Unfortunately, this is the highest risk out of all the mentioned strategies, which is the reason why investors should be careful not to invest too much money in these funds even though high rewards are also possible if things work out.

Short Selling

This is the strategy that Melvin Capital and other hedge funds involved in the GameStop (GME) event used.

Even though Ryan Cohen (Chewy CEO and co-founder) and two former associates joined the GameStop board and had spent millions in the company which caused the stock price to rebound, several hedge funds and other institutional investors continued to short-sell its stock. This action was said to be an attempt by big players to dominate amateur traders to influence and persuade panic selling. At the same time, the WSB Reddit community saw this as an opportunity to fight against the big players by joining forces to create a major short squeeze which they successfully did.

Melvin Capital and Citron Research were some of the short-sellers impacted by this event. Luckily, Citadel and Point27 Asset Management helped save Melvin Capital from its losses with a $2.75 billion bailout.

Let's learn more about some of the involved companies and their founders:

Melvin Capital - Gabriel Plotkin

Gabriel Plotkin runs Melvin Capital Management, a New York City-based hedge fund founded in 2014. In 2017, he ranked #20 on Forbes highest-earning hedge fund managers with $300 million earnings. During the same year, Melvin Capital posted returns of 41% net of fees.

According to their company's website, Melvin Capital uses a fundamental research-driven process to identify investments employing a long-short equity strategy.

In January 2021, the value of their assets dropped by 53 percent after betting against GameStop. But their firm's fate changed a bit when they received a $2.75 billion bailout from two industry giants.

Despite their help, Melvin Capital still reportedly lost a total of $4.55 billion in assets. This loss placed enormous pressure on them and other shorters to think twice before betting against GameStop and other assets.

After this fiasco, small-time traders at r/WallStreetBets have also turned their attention to other underdog stocks like Silver, AMC, and BlackBerry, among others.

Point 72 Asset Management - Steven Cohen

Steven Cohen is the founder of Point 72 Asset Management and the now-defunct SAC Capital Advisors (due to insider trading allegations). According to their website, their mission is to be the industry's premier asset management firm through delivering superior risk-adjusted returns, adhering to the highest ethical standards, and offering the greatest opportunities to the industry's brightest talent.

After suffering losses in January 2021, Point 72 managed to raise $1.5 billion from investors by increasing the assets of a hedge fund under management. Cohen also provided emergency funding worth $750 million to Gabriel Plotkin (his former protege) after Melvin Capital lost billions by betting against GameStop.

The Billionaire and New York Mets owner has since then taken a break from Twitter after his family started getting personal threats. Aside from Citadel, they were also accused by social media users of protecting their interests with stock-trading apps like Robinhood after they limited trading on heavily shorted stocks like GameStop.

Citron Research - Andrew Left

Citron Research is one of the longest-running stock commentary websites. Its founder, short-seller Andrew Left, has been publishing columns for 17+ years and its website's goal has always been to provide truthful information in an entertaining format to the investing public. However, Left announced in a YouTube video (published on January 29, 2021) that they are longer going to publish short-selling research and will shift to writing about companies that are worth buying instead.

Ever since his public skepticism about GameStop Corp. shares, Left has been the target of anger and backlash from stock traders to the point that certain attacks on him turned personal. Some created a fake Tinder account, while another person hacked some of his social media accounts. Someone even showed up at his doorstep and delivered pizza for him even though he hasn't ordered any.

Citadel & Citadel Securities - Kevin Griffin

These companies are founded by Kevin Griffin and they operate independently of each other. Citadel operates as a hedge fund that invested $2 billion to help Melvin Capital, while Citadel Securities plays a key role in trading across public and international stock markets as they pay online brokerages like Robinhood to handle their orders.

Even though small investors had united online to skyrocket certain stocks, Citadel still benefited from this frenzy. They were still able to make money by selling stocks slightly higher than what other people were willing to buy them. The difference is usually just a fraction of a penny per share, but this money adds up especially if repeated millions of times in a day.

The influx of newbie traders is one of the reasons for their growth since many people are stuck at home and want to earn extra money. So, it's not surprising that a lot of people are easily lured to sign up because of the little to no commission trades that these trading apps offer.

Senvest Management - Richard Mashaal And Brian Gonick

Unlike Melvin Capital and other hedge funds who lost a lot of money, a few hedge funds benefited from this frenzy. One of them is Senvest Management, a firm that earned nearly $700 million by selling its 5% stake after Elon Musk's "GameStonk" tweet which extended the short squeeze.

The owners aren't Reddit day traders or Discord users, but they started buying GME shares in September 2020 after CEO George Sherman's completing presentation and Chewy founder Ryan Cohen's investment.

GME has since become their most profitable investment by dollars earned.

Blackrock - Laurence Fink

Aside from Senvest Management, BlackRock, the world's largest provider of exchange-traded funds, also benefited after an epic short squeeze in GME stocks.

This huge asset management was founded by Laurence Fink (Chairman and Chief Executive Officer) and seven partners back in 1988. Their mission is to help investors build better financial futures and the firm is trusted to manage more money than any other investment company in the world.

According to reports, the firm revealed in a regulatory filing that it owned 13% (about 9.2 million shares) of GME at the end of 2020. This has set them up to potentially made $2.6 billion worth of profit if there's no change in their position.

CHAPTER VI

*WallStreetBets Vocabulary +
Famous People Who Spoke
Out On Social Media*

SpaceX and Tesla's founder Elon Musk fueled the GameStop stock fiasco when he tweeted "Gamestonks" at the time this unexpected financial shakeup was happening.

Those who aren't familiar would be confused by what he meant. Here's 43 of the most common lingo used on r/WallStreetBets.

Apes together strong / ��: An expression of solidarity when other traders pursue the same goals and targets.

Bag holder: The person who bought stock from another person at a higher price even though the stock is decreasing in value.

BTC: Stands for Bitcoin.

Bullish �� - When traders are expecting prices to rise or go up. They are typically part of the "Bull Gang" if they are feeling bullish.

Bearish - When traders are expecting prices to fall or go down. They are typically part of the "Bear Gang," if they are feeling bearish.

Buy The Fu--ing Dip or BTFD - Traders used this as a call to action when equity that has declined in price has the potential to recover from its current "dip" position.

CC: Stands for a credit card.

Fa---ts Delight or FD - This is an "out of the money" or "at the money" option that involves a big amount of money on soon to expire contracts. It is considered an "FD" if the bet is crazy.

$BECKY ��♀ - These are securities that white college girls love like Etsy, Lululemon, Athletica, Ulta Beauty, and Starbucks.

Diamond Hands �� �� - **When** traders are determined to hold onto their stocks or securities for as long as it takes until profit is obtained.

Discord - A messaging application that allows users to talk to other users in real-time.

Double Down or DD - When traders throw all their stock money on the table when a stock is promising and shows bright potential.

DRP - Stands for Dividend reinvestment plan.

Due Diligence or DD - This is the act of doing research or posting well-researched posts on WSB.

EF - Stands for the emergency fund.

FIRE / FI - Financially Independent, Retire Early. A group of people who plan to invest at least half of their take-home pay.

FU Fund: F--k you fund - A savings pool that traders can fall back to in case they quit their jobs.

Gains/Loss porn: Posting screenshots/positions of extreme gains or losses.

Gay bears / ���� – Short-sellers or those people who short companies and profiting off when their stocks go down.

GME �� �� - "GameStop" stocks.

GUH – Used as an exclamation for a major loss. For instance, Redditor u/ControlTheNarrativ made this sound after losing $45k 2 minutes into the market open.

Hold the line - When traders prefer to hold on to a stock even if it goes down in value. It can also mean HODL or Hold On For Dear Life.

Jay Powell or JPOW - Refers to the 16th Chair of the Federal Reserve.

Long - Certain stocks are trash investments and "long" gone so traders should sell these stocks or not buy them in the first place.

Long as a python - When traders have a large holding in one company despite the risks.

Mooning - A term used when stock or cryptocurrency has reached its peak.

Nocoiner - A term used when referring to someone who does not own any cryptocurrency.

Options - The options that traders have when it comes to investing (either buy or sell).

Paper Hands or Weak Hands �� �� - When traders sell their stocks and securities before they reach maximum profits.

Pump and Dump - When traders pump or hype certain stocks with no real data to back them up. Once these stock prices are driven up, they are typically sold or "Dumped" for profit.

$ROPE – Suicide or big losses.

Short - It means short-term investment. When traders on Reddit tell you to "short" a stock, you should buy a good amount of it because they believe that those stocks would skyrocket soon.

"Sir, this is a casino" – The right way to look at this.

Small-cap/medium cap/large cap - Refers to the total market capitalization of a company.

Stonks �� - "Stocks" intentionally misspelled and originated from "The Stonks Meme Guy" or "The Stonks Meme Man." In other contexts, it also means a stock going up that's worth watching if used with the side eyes emoji (stonks ��)

Swaggy Stocks - A website that specializes in WSB analytics tracking with organized charters and graphs that are easy to use and access.

Team Death Match or TDM = To determine who gets to ring the NYSE bell, traditional brokers fight in a TDM or a blood ring.

Tendies �� - Gains or profits.

Threatening Downward Movement or TDM - When traders believe that a stock is bound to plummet and that it will be best to sell these no matter what positions they have on it.

To The Moon or Rocket To The Moon ����� - When traders believe that a stock's price will spike, surge or skyrocket in overall value.

You Live Only Once or YOLO - When traders risk their portfolio on one single stock or options trade.

Your wife's bf – Typically used to poke at users who spend so much time on stocks that their wives might get boyfriends.

Whale / ��: Refers to someone who owns a lot of a stock or cryptocurrency.

Famous People Who Spoke Out On Twitter During the GME-Wall Street War

From Elon Musk sharing his opinion about hedge funds that short companies to John Stewart who joined Twitter to share his support to Redditors taking on Wall Street hedge funds, here are some of the best celebrity reactions related to this David and Goliath story of the modern age.

Mark Cuban - @mcuban

I got to say I LOVE LOVE what is going on with #wallstreetbets. All of those years of High-Frequency Traders front running retail traders, now speed and density of information and retail trading is giving the little guy an edge. Even my 11 yr old traded w them and made $

Original tweet link: https://twitter.com/mcuban/status/1354613692239925249

A High-frequency trading (HFT) is a computer-backed program that uses complex algorithms for data analysis and trade order fulfillments in a quick manner. Also known as algo or algorithmic trading, this trading type doesn't execute a set order, uses the speed of rules-based type of decision-making, and often looks for small trading opportunities to make profits at the expense of slow individual investors.

Mark Cuban knows that HFT gives institutional traders an advantage over retail traders, which is what motivated the Reddit community to push back against a system that doesn't have their best interest at heart.

Elon Musk - @elonmusk

Gamestonk!!

Original tweet link: https://twitter.com/elonmusk/status/1354174279894642703

u can't sell houses u don't own
u can't sell cars u don't own
but
u *can* sell stock u don't own!?

this is bs – shorting is a scam
legal only for vestigial reasons

Original tweet link: https://twitter.com/elonmusk/status/1354890601649610753

Elon Musk is one of the richest people in the world and based on his tweet above, he is not a fan of short-sellers, partly due to Tesla having its fair share of run-ins with short sellers in the past. This experience had prompted him to make Tesla private three years ago.

Morgan Housel - @morganhousel

The GameStop thing is a reminder that investing is not the study of finance. It's the study of how people behave with money, and sometimes those behaviors are incredible.

Original tweet link: https://twitter.com/morganhousel/status/1354132650244460544

This shakeup only proves that investing is still a very human activity despite the technology that powers the financial markets.

Tyler Winklevoss - @tyler

Robinhood was never what it pretended to be. It built its business on selling Wall Street Bets order flow to the hedge fund Citadel. In the moment of truth, we learned which customer it cares about the most.

Original tweet link: https://twitter.com/tyler/status/1354812210481008640

Many people were furious when Robinhood temporarily halted GME stock purchases while still allowing for liquidations. This move revealed their true colors and people soon realized that it's not the kind of trading platform they originally thought.

Chamath Palihapitiya - @chamath

In moments of uncertainty, when courage and strength are required, you find out who the true corporatist scumbags are.

Original tweet link: https://twitter.com/chamath/status/1354840270064377858

This fiasco happened for a reason and that is to let us know about what the elites have been doing all along.

Dan Price - @DanPriceSeattle

Stock market hits record highs at a time of record lines for food banks
"well, the rich just know how to invest"

Regular people game the same system through GameStop
"We must stop this immediately"

Original tweet link: https://twitter.com/DanPriceSeattle/status/1354495099665846275

Isn't it ironic how big players suddenly don't want the little players to join the game?

Kevin O'Leary - @kevinolearytv

Old days where a hedge fund manager could quietly short a stock, then publish negative research and take a bullhorn to it in the media are over. They now run the risk that the power of the crowd will turn on them and squeeze their heads like a teenage pimple. I'm good with it!

Original tweet link: https://twitter.com/kevinolearytv/status/1354788578316988417

O'Leary knows that market manipulations have been going on for ages. Gone are the days when only the big players have their shot at the game.

Pat McAfee - @PatMcAfeeShow

So what happens next?? They freeze everybody's accounts. Lawsuits happen... They never end.. #WallStreetBets goes into hiding... Dogecoin goes to the moon.. the world goes on??

Original tweet link: https://twitter.com/PatMcAfeeShow/status/1354993600585728003

McAfee's tweet above does make sense. Where do we go from here after the collective buying power of retail traders shook Wall Street? We can't exactly predict what the future holds, but one thing is for sure! Hedge funds have to think twice now before shorting stocks of seemingly fading companies.

Jon Stewart - @jonstewart

This is bullsh-t. The Redditors aren't cheating, they're joining a party Wall Street insiders have been enjoying for years. Don't shut them down...maybe sue them for copyright infringement instead!!
We've learned nothing from 2008.

Love
StewBeef

Original tweet link: https://twitter.com/jonstewart/status/1354901018564321287

Comedian and former "Daily Show" host Jon Stewart voiced his support to Redditors because why not?

Alexandria Ocasio-Cortez - @AOC

We now need to know more about @RobinhoodApp's decision to block retail investors from purchasing stock while hedge funds are freely able to trade the stock as they see fit.

As a member of the Financial Services Cmte, I'd support a hearing if necessary.

Original tweet link: https://twitter.com/tedcruz/

status/1354833603943931905

Stopping retail traders from purchasing GME stocks sparked outrage among lawmakers, including Rep. Alexandria Ocasio-Cortez, D-N.Y. Even Sen. Ted Cruz, R-Texas agreed with what she tweeted.

Robin Hood - @robinhood

Lovely to have all these new followers ... can we just check that you know that you're following The World Wide Robin Hood Society in Nottingham and not the Robin Hood App... if so .. a big welcome from Sherwood.

Original tweet link: https://twitter.com/robinhood/status/1354786505873625091

During this fiasco, the Twitter account of the World Wide Robin Hood Society in the U.K gained about 40,000 followers. Many social media users mistook the account which promotes the actual Robin Hood legend as the account of the Robinhood app.

CHAPTER VII

*WallStreetBets & The Future
Of Trading*

There's no denying that trading is getting a lot more attention after the decentralized WallStreetBets Reddit forum caused chaos on Wall Street.

While there is still plenty of this story left to play out, this shakeup in the financial world means it will change the way investors perceive the market, its participants, and its rules, as well as shape future rules and regulations going forward.

Trading will never be the same again as the rise of trading information and apps emerge. As market prices move, trading strategies get affected, and more and more people become aware of what the hedge funds have been doing, it's safe to say that this isn't going to be the last time the WSB Reddit forum members will be taking down the big boys.

There will be a lot of awesome trading opportunities in the future but is the reward always greater than the risk? Short selling has always been a very risky investment strategy because the risk increases as time goes by. The WSB forum members will still hold on to the position to achieve their end goal despite the potential risk or "diamond hands" as they say it in WSB lingo.

The reality is that this short squeeze won't last forever, and the real value of GameStop and other shorted stocks will reassert in one way or another. "Diamond hands" isn't going to work out all the time and timing is very important to benefit from driving up the stock price of certain stocks.

Taxes - Wall Street-Gme Edition

If you're one of the retail investors who made a lot of moolah on GameStop stocks, there's one catch: hefty capital gains taxes. However, fret not because taxes that occurred in January 2021 wouldn't be due until April 2022.

Whether you're a newbie trader or a seasoned trader, don't be tempted to spend all your money once you cash in on your gains. Put some aside and put it to good use so that it'll grow and you can pay the taxes you owe the government before the deadline. The rates will vary depending on your income and filing status and a professional accountant can help you sort things out.